MAJOR LEAGUE BASEBALL'S
TOP 50

Written by the Editors of Major League Baseball

MAJOR LEAGUE BASEBALL PROPERTIES, INC.

CONTENTS

Major League Baseball's Top 50 was developed, written and designed by MLB PUBLISHING, the publishing department of Major League Baseball Properties, Inc.

Printed in the U.S.A.

First Printing: August 2007

ISBN-13: 978-0-9776476-2-0
ISBN-10: 0-9776476-2-5

Photo Credits © MLB Photos Williamson (Pujols p. 4, Santana p. 7, Oswalt p. 14, Teixeira p. 26, Papelbon p. 27, Hernandez p. 35, Beckett p. 37, Varitek p. 39); Grieshop (Pujols p. 5 (r), Cabrera p. 9, Berkman p. 22, Zambrano p. 26); Pilling (A. Rodriguez p. 6, Reyes p. 8, Howard p. 10, M. Ramirez p. 10, Soriano p. 13, Jones p. 14, Wells p. 15, Jeter p. 16, Rivera p. 20, Tejada p. 25, Utley p. 26, H. Ramirez p. 28, Bay p. 29, Beltran p. 39); Leiter (Beltran p. 8, Rollins p. 30 and 31, Hoffman p. 32, Holliday p. 34); Sanford (Halladay p. 15); Shamus (Hafner p. 20); Reid (Morneau p. 22, Nathan p. 24); Zagaris (Bonds p. 29, Swisher p. 42); Daniel (Lee p. 32, Griffey p. 33); Schechter (Willis p. 32); Kluckhorn (Hunter p. 33); Vesely (Mauer p. 17, Sizemore p. 19); Spinelli (Guerrero p. 39); Cunningham (I. Rodriguez p. 43); Mangin (Guerrero p. 9, Crawford p. 11, Webb p. 23, AT&T Park p. 40). **© Getty Images** Elsa (Carpenter p. 20, Beckett p. 36, Ortiz p. 41); Fiume (Sizemore p. 18); Schechter (Ortiz p. 9); McIsaac (Soriano p. 12, Jeter p. 43); Greule Jr. (Suzuki p. 17); Bello (Wright p. 21, Zito p. 40); Petersen (F. Rodriguez p. 24); Vishwanat (Pujols p. 5 (l), A. Ramirez p. 35); Jacobsohn (Zito p. 35); Jasienski (Peavy p. 17); Serota (Tejada p. 42); Babineau/Getty Images (Schilling p. 34).

Who's No. 1? While we're at it, who's No. 17, 22 or 43?

Baseball is and always has been about making lists. Back in the 1920s, fans debated who was better: Babe Ruth or Ty Cobb. In the 1940s, you were either a Ted Williams or Joe DiMaggio fan. During the 1980 World Series between the Royals and Phillies, all fans wanted to talk about was which team's third baseman was better — George Brett or Mike Schmidt.

How do today's players stack up? Which guys will you be talking about for years to come? Does Travis Hafner rank higher than Roy Halladay? What about Ichiro vs. David Wright?

Hopefully you can spend plenty of time creating your own list. But what follows is ours. So turn the page and start comparing.

POSITION: First Base **TEAM:** St. Louis Cardinals **THROWS:** Right **BATS:** Right **UNIFORM #:** 5

STAT CHART

Albert's first six seasons were incredible. Here's how they compare to two all-time greats:
ALBERT PUJOLS (2001–06):
.332 AVG, 250 HR, 758 RBI
JOE DiMAGGIO (1936–41):
.345 AVG, 198 HR, 816 RBI
TED WILLIAMS (1939–42, 46–47):
.352 AVG, 197 HR, 752 RBI

Albert Pujols doesn't need a catchy nickname or his own clothing line. His incredible skills alone have made him one of the most famous athletes on the planet. But it's his tireless work ethic and desire to constantly keep improving that have put him in a class by himself. Before turning 27, Pujols won Rookie of the Year, MVP and Gold Glove awards, a batting title and — most importantly — a World Series ring. Since coming to America from the Dominican Republic when he was a young boy, Pujols has dedicated himself to being the best he can be both on and off the field. "I think he distinguishes himself every day," says Cardinals Manager Tony La Russa.

"One of the reasons I respect Albert so much is that he is dedicated to helping his club [win the World Series]. It hasn't been about stats; it hasn't been about money. This guy is a winning player. He's going to be out there trying hard."

—Tony La Russa

When A-Rod gets hot, no one is better. Since making his Big League debut with Seattle as an 18-year-old shortstop in 1994, Alex has proven to be one of the game's greatest all-around players, and one of its most feared sluggers. In 2006, he became the youngest player ever to reach 450 home runs. He may have the largest contract in baseball history, but A-Rod still has that kid inside him, the one who jumped up and down on the bed and hit his head on the ceiling when the ball went through Bill Buckner's legs in the 1986 World Series. "Why do I play baseball?" he says. "Because I love it. Making money doesn't mean your passion stops."

factoid

As a kid, A-Rod was a big collector of baseball cards. So he was pretty thrilled when the Topps company asked him to be its first official spokesman in 2004.

MAGIC NUMBER

57

A-Rod's homers in 2002 — the most ever by a shortstop.

POSITION: Third Base
TEAM: New York Yankees
THROWS: Right
BATS: Right
UNIFORM #: 13

⅃ JOHANSANTANA

POSITION: Pitcher **TEAM:** Minnesota Twins **THROWS:** Left **BATS:** Left **UNIFORM #:** 57

> **"When Johan is on the mound, he exudes so much confidence that we kind of feed off that, and we go out there and play with that same confidence. So it's a huge boost for us, especially in the Metrodome, because we feel like he is going to go out there and dominate."**
>
> **—Michael Cuddyer**

Looking at what Johan Santana has done in recent years, it's hard to believe that not one, but *two* teams passed up on him earlier in his career. After originally being signed by the Astros in 1995, the Marlins picked him up virtually free of charge in the 1999 Rule 5 Draft. Florida then traded Johan to Minnesota, where he has been nothing short of unstoppable. The Venezuelan left-hander won his second Cy Young Award in 2006 — the only pitcher in Twins history with more than one. With a fastball that reaches the mid-90s and a mid-70s change-up, Santana can fool even the best hitters. "Right now, he is the best pitcher in the game," says Blue Jays designated hitter Frank Thomas. "Typically, he never makes many mistakes."

4 JOSE REYES

POSITION: Shortstop **TEAM:** New York Mets **THROWS:** Right **BATS:** Switch **UNIFORM #:** 7

STAT CHART

Here's how Jose's first 500 games compare to those of another great leadoff hitter, Rickey Henderson:

REYES (2003–07):	HENDERSON (1979–82):
347 R, 48 3B, 191 SB	365 R, 18 3B, 315 SB

Major Leaguers are fans, too, and if you ask them what player they would pay to see, their answer is almost always the same: Jose Reyes. The speedy leadoff man dazzles on the field, turning doubles into triples, stealing bases and scoring runs. Thanks to his strong arm, Reyes also is one of the game's best shortstops. "The guy who can take over the game the fastest is Jose Reyes," says catcher Paul Lo Duca. "He's the most exciting player, and he can be dominant."

5 CARLOSBELTRAN

POSITION: Center Field **TEAM:** New York Mets **THROWS:** Right **BATS:** Switch **UNIFORM #:** 15

From the graceful way he covers the outfield to his sweet, powerful swing at the plate, Carlos Beltran makes it look so easy. "He can do a little bit of everything," says teammate Tom Glavine. "Those guys are nice to have on your side." The Mets signed Beltran as a free agent after his stellar performance in the 2004 playoffs with Houston, when he hit eight homers in 12 games. He has been clutch in New York, too, hitting three homers in the '06 NLCS.

> **Honestly, I think that Carlos being labeled as a 30/30 guy might be a bit of an understatement.**
> —David Wright

6 DAVID ORTIZ

POSITION: Designated Hitter
TEAM: Boston Red Sox
THROWS: Left **BATS:** Left
UNIFORM #: 34

Since signing with the Red Sox in 2003, "Big Papi" has evolved into one of the game's scariest hitters, as well as one of its most clutch performers. He blasted nine walk-off homers in his first four seasons with Boston, including two in the 2004 playoffs. "When you can come through in those kinds of situations, people really appreciate it," Ortiz says. "It takes a lot of concentration. I guess it's been working the right way for me, and I'm going to try to keep it that way."

factoid

While some stars have had candy bars named after them, Ortiz might be the first with his own sauce, called "Ortiz's Corn & Black Bean Big Papi Salsa."

7 VLADIMIR GUERRERO

POSITION: Right Field **TEAM:** Los Angeles Angels of Anaheim **THROWS:** Right **BATS:** Right **UNIFORM #:** 27

Vladi has been punishing AL pitchers for so long some people forget he was a four-time All-Star with the Expos. But all it takes is one game to remember just how dominant he is. Able to crush almost any pitch even *near* the strike zone, the 2004 AL MVP has never hit below .300 in a full season. Former teammate Darin Erstad put it best: "He's one of those guys that you're going to tell your grandkids about."

8 MIGUEL CABRERA

POSITION: Third Base **TEAM:** Florida Marlins **THROWS:** Right **BATS:** Right **UNIFORM #:** 24

Cabrera made his debut in June of 2003 at the age of 20. Four months later, he was a world champion. In the three seasons that followed, Cabrera averaged more than 30 home runs and 114 RBI. "He's so advanced and disciplined for a hitter at his young age," says fellow NL East third baseman David Wright. "He torments us every time we play him. I kind of wish that he wasn't in our division."

MAGIC NUMBER

.339

Cabrera's franchise-record batting average in 2006.

9 RYAN HOWARD

After winning Minor League MVP awards in 2003 and '04, Ryan Howard became the target of many teams looking to trade for him. Luckily for the Phillies, they held on to their supersized slugger and have been greatly rewarded. Howard was the NL Rookie of the Year in 2005, then took home MVP honors in '06 — the first player since Cal Ripken to win those two awards in his first two seasons. His terrific 2006 was highlighted by 58 regular-season homers — the most ever for a second-year player — and his first Home Run Derby crown.

> **He's got so much opposite power. Not many guys can go opposite field with that much power.**
>
> —Chase Utley

POSITION: First Base
TEAM: Philadelphia Phillies
THROWS: Left **BATS:** Left
UNIFORM #: 6

10 MANNY RAMIREZ

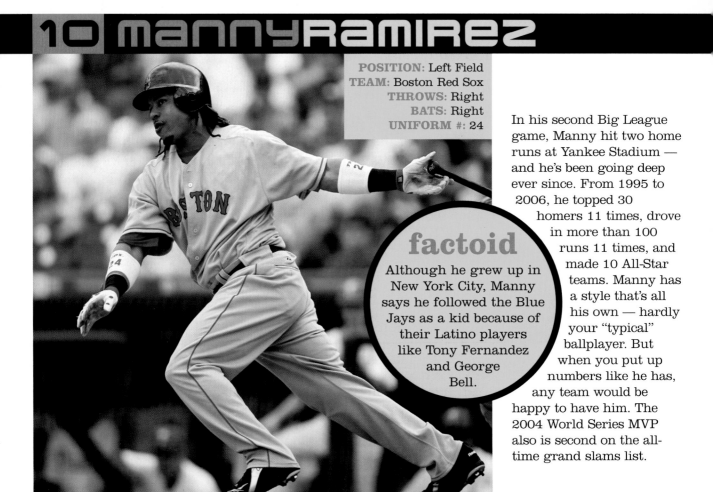

POSITION: Left Field
TEAM: Boston Red Sox
THROWS: Right
BATS: Right
UNIFORM #: 24

In his second Big League game, Manny hit two home runs at Yankee Stadium — and he's been going deep ever since. From 1995 to 2006, he topped 30 homers 11 times, drove in more than 100 runs 11 times, and made 10 All-Star teams. Manny has a style that's all his own — hardly your "typical" ballplayer. But when you put up numbers like he has, any team would be happy to have him. The 2004 World Series MVP also is second on the all-time grand slams list.

factoid

Although he grew up in New York City, Manny says he followed the Blue Jays as a kid because of their Latino players like Tony Fernandez and George Bell.

POSITION: Left Field **TEAM:** Tampa Bay Devil Rays **THROWS:** Left **BATS:** Left **UNIFORM #:** 13

factoid

Like fellow MLB Top 50 players Dontrelle Willis and Jimmy Rollins, Carl participated in the Reviving Baseball in Inner Cities (RBI) program as a kid.

The Rays knew Crawford was a multi-talented athlete when they drafted him out of high school in 1999. He was recruited to play basketball for UCLA after scoring 25.0 points per game as a senior, and also was offered a scholarship to play football at Nebraska. What the team didn't expect was how much Crawford would improve. He is just the second player in history to increase his batting average and home run totals in five straight seasons, and he's on pace to join Ty Cobb as the only players to reach 1,000 hits, 300 steals and 100 triples before the age of 28.

STAT CHART

	AVG	HR	SB	3B
2002:	.259	2	9	6
2003:	.281	5	55	9
2004:	.296	11	59	19
2005:	.301	15	46	15
2006:	.305	18	58	16

POSITION: Outfield
TEAM: Chicago Cubs
THROWS: Right
BATS: Right
UNIFORM #: 12

> **A**s I was rounding the bases, I was thinking about my family in the Dominican Republic who was watching the game, because they could not be here with me. I was hoping they were watching it and enjoying it.
>
> —Alfonso Soriano, after hitting a walk-off home run at Yankee Stadium in the 2001 ALCS

DIAMOND LINGO

Big Leaguers have their own unique way of calling the action on the field. Here are a few terms that Alfonso loves to hear:

dinger: a home run
meatball: an easy pitch to hit
tools: a player's set of skills
wheels: a ballplayer's legs

Manager Lou Piniella has had some terrific ballplayers play for him — A-Rod, Ken Griffey Jr. and Carl Crawford, to name a few. Now, as manager of the Cubs, he gets to work with another awesome talent: Alfonso Soriano. "I mean this guy here has got just a special combination of speed and power," Piniella says. That certainly was true in 2006, when Sori became the first player in history to hit 40 homers, 40 doubles and steal 40 bases in the same season. Like many of MLB's Top 50, Soriano came from a humble background, and even though he's now a big star, he never forgets where he came from. "Everything I do in baseball is dedicated to my mother back in the Dominican Republic," he says.

13 ANDRUW JONES

POSITION: Center Field **TEAM:** Atlanta Braves **THROWS:** Right **BATS:** Right **UNIFORM #:** 25

Growing up on the Caribbean island of Curaçao, Andruw would swing a sledgehammer like a baseball bat to help strengthen his wrists. The training paid off in 1996, when he became the youngest player ever to hit a home run in a World Series. He has since become one of Atlanta's all-time greats, with more than 350 career homers and nine Gold Gloves.

DO THE MATH

Figuring out Jones' batting average or Oswalt's ERA is a lot easier than you might think.
BATTING AVERAGE (AVG): number of hits divided by at-bats
EARNED RUN AVERAGE (ERA): earned runs allowed times nine, divided by innings pitched

14 ROY OSWALT

POSITION: Pitcher
TEAM: Houston Astros
THROWS: Right
BATS: Right
UNIFORM #: 44

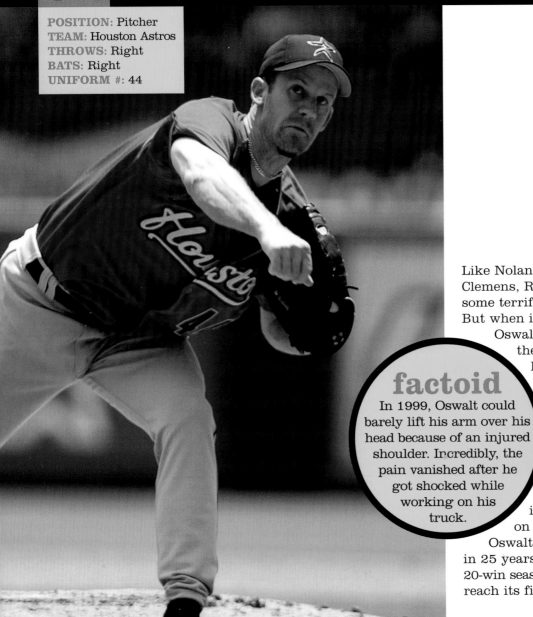

factoid
In 1999, Oswalt could barely lift his arm over his head because of an injured shoulder. Incredibly, the pain vanished after he got shocked while working on his truck.

Like Nolan Ryan and Roger Clemens, Roy Oswalt has had some terrific seasons in Houston. But when it comes to being a star, Oswalt prefers to stay out of the spotlight. "He just likes going out and pitching, doing his job and saying 'Thank you very much' and going on home," says Astros Manager Phil Garner. But that doesn't mean the quiet Mississippian isn't an absolute bulldog on the mound. In 2005, Oswalt became the first Astro in 25 years to post back-to-back 20-win seasons and helped Houston reach its first World Series.

POSITION: Center Field **TEAM:** Toronto Blue Jays **THROWS:** Right **BATS:** Right **UNIFORM #:** 10

The story goes like this: One day during Little League practice, a ground ball skipped up and smacked young Vernon Wells right in the face. Vernon concluded after that incident that he wanted to give the outfield a try — a decision that would eventually make him an All-Star in the Major Leagues. In 2004, Wells played 130 games in center field for the Blue Jays and made just one error, winning his first Gold Glove Award. The next year, he played in 153 games without a single error! Vernon is more than just a slick fielder, though — in 2003, he led the Majors with 215 hits.

factoid

Vernon may look like he's all business, but he's actually one of the bigger jokesters in the game, known for putting shaving cream pies in guys' faces.

After being drafted out of Arvada (CO) West High School in 1995, Roy Halladay was called up at the end of the 1998 season and soon showed the Blue Jays just what kind of pitcher they had. In his second career start, he had a no-hitter going until a pinch-hitter homered with two outs in the ninth. Halladay hung on for the complete-game victory that day — a stat that would become his trademark. "Doc," as he is known, works quickly and isn't afraid to go all nine. Of his 22 wins in 2003, when he won his first AL Cy Young Award, eight were complete games.

> **The way he's gone out and dominated, I felt wholeheartedly that Roy should have started. He's the best pitcher in the league.**
>
> —Mark Buehrle, at the 2005 All-Star Game

POSITION: Pitcher
TEAM: Toronto Blue Jays
THROWS: Right
BATS: Right
UNIFORM #: 32

16 ROY HALLADAY

POSITION:	Shortstop
TEAM:	New York Yankees
THROWS:	Right
BATS:	Right
UNIFORM #:	2

When Derek Jeter's career comes to an end, there will be many ways of recognizing what a great player he was. But to measure Jeter's full value, you have to look beyond the awards and the statistics. "He can do it all," says fellow perennial All-Star Ichiro Suzuki. "There is no one part of his game you can focus on stopping." When Alex Rodriguez joined the Yankees, he said: "Derek does it all with grace and elegance." Jeter's smooth defense, his knack for coming up huge in the clutch, his leadership on and off the field, all ensure that the Yankee captain's legacy will last forever.

"Being a leader is not something I think about. I try to lead by example, by playing hard."

—Derek Jeter

18 ICHIRO SUZUKI

After winning seven consecutive batting titles and seven straight Gold Glove Awards in Japan, Ichiro became the first Japanese position player to sign with a Major League club. His lethal combo of speed, instincts and overall skills led him to become the second player ever to win Rookie of the Year and MVP honors in the same season (2001). "He can hit anything," says Andy Pettitte. "You just have to hope he hits it up in the air, because he's so fast he beats out ground balls." In his first six Big League seasons, Ichiro won six Gold Gloves and made six All-Star teams. In 2004, he set a single-season record with 262 hits.

POSITION: Center Field
TEAM: Seattle Mariners
THROWS: Right **BATS:** Left
UNIFORM #: 51

19 JAKE PEAVY

POSITION: Pitcher **TEAM:** San Diego Padres **THROWS:** Right **BATS:** Right **UNIFORM #:** 44

How's this for intimidating: Jake Peavy can blow away hitters with his fastball, make them swing and miss with his slider, or buckle their knees with a change-up — and he's legally blind! Thanks to strong contact lenses, however, Peavy still has pinpoint accuracy. In 2004, he led the NL in ERA; in 2005, he led the league in strikeouts; and in both 2006 and 2007, he struck out 16 batters in one game. "He has the ability to be one of the best starting pitchers in the National League, year in and year out," says Padres Manager Bud Black. Cardinals Manager Tony La Russa agrees: "This guy is the real deal. Great competitor."

20 JOE MAUER

POSITION: Catcher **TEAM:** Minnesota Twins **THROWS:** Right **BATS:** Left **UNIFORM #:** 7

Minnesota has known Joe Mauer for a while. He was born in St. Paul, played high school baseball (as well as football and basketball) at Cretin-Derham Hall there, and now stars for the Twins. The 6-foot-5 Mauer, who was the first pick in the 2001 MLB First-Year Player Draft, has lived up to expectations, and in 2006 became the first catcher ever to win an AL batting title.

factoid
Mauer tied a national high school record by blasting a home run in seven consecutive games. He also struck out just once in his entire high school career!

Whether the Indians are ahead or behind, heading toward the playoffs or heading home, Grady Sizemore plays the same way every day: with 100 percent, all-out effort. He'll routinely dive into walls to catch fly balls or turn on the speedburners to beat out infield grounders in meaningless games. Thanks to Sizemore, though, Cleveland won't be playing many of those. In 2006, the Washington native became the youngest player in history with 90 extra-base hits and 20 steals in the same year.

factoid

Sizemore admits he is a germophobe who washes his hands constantly and refuses to walk around hotel rooms in bare feet. "You could get sick so easily," he says.

" All of us are fortunate to see him every day. He is one of the greatest players of our generation. "

—Indians General Manager Mark Shapiro in the
May 14, 2007, issue of *Sports Illustrated*

22 TRAVIS HAFNER

POSITION: Designated Hitter **TEAM:** Cleveland Indians **THROWS:** Right **BATS:** Left **UNIFORM #:** 48

He may not have the same speed as teammate Grady Sizemore, but Travis Hafner usually doesn't have to rush to home plate. The Indians' designated hitter is a home run machine, displaying his power by smashing 103 dingers from 2004 to '06. The man they call "Pronk" (a combination of "The Project" and "Donkey") played several sports in high school, and he still enjoys watching WWE wrestling on television.

STAT CHART

Hafner's numbers have risen steadily since he debuted in '02.

	AVG	HR	RBI
2002:	.242	1	6
2003:	.254	14	40
2004:	.311	28	109
2005:	.305	33	108
2006:	.308	42	117

23 MARIANO RIVERA

POSITION: Pitcher **TEAM:** New York Yankees **THROWS:** Right **BATS:** Right **UNIFORM #:** 42

factoid

The only player who wears No. 42 regularly, Rivera is the last player remaining who has worn the number since it was retired as a tribute to Jackie Robinson in 1997.

Regarded by many as the greatest relief pitcher ever, Mo has dominated hitters since becoming the Yankees' full-time closer in 1997. While he averages more than 40 saves per year during the regular season, it's under the intense pressure of the playoffs that Rivera's star shines brightest. Through 2006, Mo had recorded a 0.80 ERA and 34 saves (19 more than the next closest guy, Dennis Eckersley) in postseason play — both of which are Major League records.

24 CHRIS CARPENTER

POSITION: Pitcher **TEAM:** St. Louis Cardinals **THROWS:** Right **BATS:** Right **UNIFORM #:** 29

A first-round pick of the Blue Jays in 1993, Carpenter spent six mostly forgettable years in Toronto, compiling a 49-50 record and an ERA near 5.00. Despite knowing that he would need more than a year off to recover from shoulder surgery, the Cardinals took a chance on the right-hander when few other teams would. The payoff has been huge. In 2004, Carpenter went 15-5 and pitched St. Louis into the World Series. He followed that up with a 21-5 campaign in 2005 that netted him his first NL Cy Young Award. "He's fearless out there," says teammate Jason Isringhausen. "He doesn't back down from anything."

> ❝**If** you're a parent, you want your son to turn out the way David did.❞
>
> —former teammate Doug Mientkiewicz

factoid

David's diving, bare-handed catch with his back to the infield against the Padres on Aug. 9, 2005, was voted the Play of the Year on MLB.com.

When the Mets drafted David Wright out of Hickory (VA) High School in 2001, they got more than just a talented infielder who could hit home runs and drive in more than 100 runs every year. They got a young player capable of being a true team leader — that rare guy who can lift a team's spirits when the going gets tough. "I can't say enough good things about him," says former teammate Joe McEwing. "He works hard every single day, and whatever he gets, he deserves."

POSITION: Third Base
TEAM: New York Mets
THROWS: Right
BATS: Right
UNIFORM #: 5

25 DAVID WRIGHT

26 LANCE BERKMAN

POSITION: First Base
TEAM: Houston Astros
THROWS: Left **BATS:** Switch
UNIFORM #: 17

Whether he is playing the outfield, where he spent most of his time early in his career, or at first base, where he is put most often these days, Lance Berkman can swing the bat. On Sept. 13, 2006, he became only the second switch-hitter in history to hit 40 or more home runs in multiple seasons, joining Mickey Mantle, which is appropriate. "My dad was a Yankee fan," Lance says, "and he wanted me to be a switch-hitter because Mickey Mantle was his favorite player."

MAGIC NUMBER

3

Berkman's homers in the 2004 NLCS.

27 JUSTIN MORNEAU

POSITION: First Base **TEAM:** Minnesota Twins **THROWS:** Right **BATS:** Left **UNIFORM #:** 33

Morneau is one of the latest stars to come out of Minnesota's terrific Minor League system. Drafted in the third round by the Twins in 1999, Justin played in the Majors a little bit in 2003. He received more regular playing time in 2004 and '05, and showed his great ability. Then it all came together for him in 2006. Morneau, who was born in New Westminster, Canada, hit .321 with 34 home runs and a whopping 130 RBI to help Minnesota win the AL Central. For his efforts, Morneau was named the AL MVP, making him the first Canadian to receive that honor. And through the early part of 2007, he had shown no sign of stopping.

STAT CHART

Morneau has continued to improve.

	G	R	HR	RBI	AVG
2004:	74	39	19	58	.271
2005:	141	62	22	79	.239
2006:	157	97	34	130	.321

factoid

Brandon is such a star in Kentucky, his home state, that early in 2007 they named a road after him. It's part of U.S. 60 near his hometown of Ashland.

You step back into the batter's box to face Brandon Webb. Your knees are shaking. He has you down 0-2 and you're just looking for something to hit. His next pitch looks like a strike, but just as you bring the bat around, the ball drops to the dirt. It's too late to stop your swing, so the ball just dribbles out to the mound for an easy putout. Don't feel too bad, though. Nearly 9 out of 10 Big Leaguers make an out in an 0-2 count against Webb. That sinker is usually called one of the game's very best pitches. In 2006, it helped Brandon earn the NL Cy Young Award, as he won 16 games, put up a 3.10 ERA, and struck out 178 batters.

POSITION: Pitcher
TEAM: Arizona Diamondbacks
THROWS: Right
BATS: Right
UNIFORM #: 17

> "When that pitch is on, it doesn't matter if you're looking for it or not. You can go swing at it and it just disappears. It's really a one-of-a-kind sinker."
>
> —Arizona Diamondbacks Manager Bob Melvin, in the June 12, 2006, issue of *Sports Illustrated*

29 FRANCISCO RODRIGUEZ

His nickname is K-Rod (and it's not because of a love for Special K cereal). Francisco Rodriguez, the closer for the Los Angeles Angels of Anaheim, strikes people out in bunches. Entering 2007, he had put up four straight seasons with 90 or more Ks, thanks to a blazing fastball and a sharp curve. Such terrific stuff has also meant loads of saves for Rodriguez and loads of wins for the Angels. On Sept. 10, 2006, at age 24, Francisco became the youngest player ever to reach the 100-save mark. Since '02, when Rodriguez debuted, the Angels have been to the playoffs three times and won one title.

DIAMOND LINGO

If you want to talk about K-Rod the way Major Leaguers do, get to know these terms:
closer: a relief pitcher who finishes games
flame thrower: a hard-throwing pitcher
heat: a good fastball
punchout: a strikeout

POSITION: Pitcher
TEAM: Los Angeles Angels of Anaheim
THROWS: Right
BATS: Right
UNIFORM #: 57

30 JOE NATHAN

POSITION: Pitcher   **TEAM:** Minnesota Twins   **THROWS:** Right   **BATS:** Right   **UNIFORM #:** 36

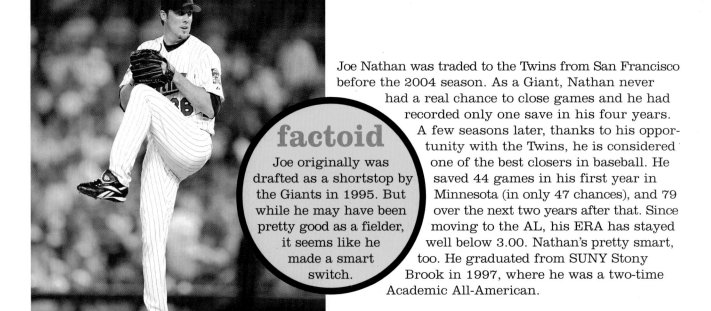

factoid
Joe originally was drafted as a shortstop by the Giants in 1995. But while he may have been pretty good as a fielder, it seems like he made a smart switch.

Joe Nathan was traded to the Twins from San Francisco before the 2004 season. As a Giant, Nathan never had a real chance to close games and he had recorded only one save in his four years. A few seasons later, thanks to his opportunity with the Twins, he is considered one of the best closers in baseball. He saved 44 games in his first year in Minnesota (in only 47 chances), and 79 over the next two years after that. Since moving to the AL, his ERA has stayed well below 3.00. Nathan's pretty smart, too. He graduated from SUNY Stony Brook in 1997, where he was a two-time Academic All-American.

POSITION: Shortstop **TEAM:** Baltimore Orioles **THROWS:** Right **BATS:** Right **UNIFORM #:** 10

factoid
As a kid in the Dominican Republic, Miguel was a huge fan of Baltimore shortstop Cal Ripken Jr. Now, Miguel plays the same position for the same team.

Watching Miguel Tejada, it's clear that he loves to play baseball. Need proof? Until an injury in 2007, he had rarely missed a game. From the middle of the 2000 season to June 21, 2007, Tejada played in 1,152 straight. And it's a good thing for the Orioles, too, because Miguel is terrific on the field. Every year, he seems to hit .300 with 30 home runs and 100 runs batted in. In 2002, he earned the AL MVP Award. Two years later, he had a league-best 150 RBI.

You can't help but love to have a guy like Miguel on your team because he brings all the intangibles that you look for. He's always pumped and he plays every day.

—former teammate B.J. Ryan

32 CHASE UTLEY

POSITION: Second Base **TEAM:** Philadelphia Phillies **THROWS:** Right **BATS:** Left **UNIFORM #:** 26

Utley's first Big League hit was a grand slam, a fitting way for the Phillies' standout second baseman to start his career. He originally was a part-time player in Philly, sharing time with Placido Polanco, but when given the full-time starting job, he didn't disappoint. In 2006 — just his second full season in the Major Leagues — Utley scored the most runs in the National League (131). He also got 203 hits, which was second most. Chase was voted to the All-Star Game as the NL's starting second baseman and won his first Silver Slugger Award, which is given annually to the best hitter at each position.

33 MARK TEIXEIRA

As a rookie in 2003, Teixeira had a lot of success. He hit 26 home runs and 29 doubles, and he knocked in 84 runs. He easily could have sat back and been a pretty good Major Leaguer. But Teixeira continued to work hard on all parts of his game. "I go out there and expect a lot out of myself," he says. "Numbers just kind of happen by going out there and playing every day." Thanks to his effort, the numbers have happened for him in a big way. He hit more than 30 home runs and tallied more than 100 RBI each of the next three seasons. He also has been a great defensive player, winning Gold Gloves at first base in 2005 and '06.

factoid

When he was taken by the Texas Rangers with the fifth pick of the 2001 Draft, Mark was the first of nine Georgia Tech players that were chosen that year.

POSITION: First Base
TEAM: Texas Rangers
THROWS: Right **BATS:** Switch
UNIFORM #: 23

34 CARLOS ZAMBRANO

POSITION: Pitcher **TEAM:** Chicago Cubs **THROWS:** Right **BATS:** Switch **UNIFORM #:** 38

MAGIC NUMBER

16

Big Z's wins in '06.

Carlos Zambrano has earned the nickname "Big Z" from teammates. It's not surprising, since he is 6-foot-5 and 255 lbs. Carlos also has a big personality, which you can tell by watching him pitch. He yells into his glove or into the air, he pumps his fist — anything to help him stay focused. It seems to work. He is one of only two NL pitchers to win at least 13 games each year from 2003 to '06, along with Greg Maddux.

> **I** added a split-finger to my repertoire, and that has pretty much been able to keep the hitters guessing. That's what has helped me dominate hitters.
>
> —Jonathan Papelbon

In 2006, Jonathan Papelbon was a surprise. After reasonable success in 17 games in 2005, he was off the charts as the full-time closer in '06. Papelbon recorded 20 straight saves in the team's first 52 games. He let up seven earned runs all season, in 59 appearances. "Every time he goes in, it seems like he does his job," said Neal Cotts, then a reliever with the White Sox, during the '06 season. "He hasn't failed too many times this year." The start of 2007 was similar, as Papelbon saved 16 of his first 17 chances with an ERA around 2.00.

DO THE MATH

A good measure of how effective a pitcher has been is his WHIP. It tells you how many runners the hurler has put on base. Papelbon's was 0.78 in 2006, which is excellent.

WHIP:
walks plus hits, divided by innings

POSITION: Pitcher
TEAM: Boston Red Sox
THROWS: Right
BATS: Right
UNIFORM #: 58

35 JONATHANPAPELBON

Hanley Ramirez has a solid mix of speed and power. As a rookie in 2006, he stole 51 bases, hit 17 homers and was named NL Rookie of the Year. He was the first NL rookie ever to record more than 50 steals and 110 runs. "He has the opportunity to be a complete player," says Dodgers coach Mariano Duncan, who first saw Hanley play a few years ago in the Dominican Republic. "Very few shortstops in this day have the speed he has and the power he has, with the ability to hit for average. In two or three years, you'll see him in that group with Jeter and Tejada."

MAGIC NUMBER

7

Leadoff home runs hit by Ramirez in 2006.

POSITION: Shortstop TEAM: Florida Marlins THROWS: Right BATS: Right UNIFORM #: 2

36 HANLEYRAMIREZ

37 BARRYBONDS

POSITION: Left Field TEAM: San Francisco Giants THROWS: Left BATS: Left UNIFORM #: 25

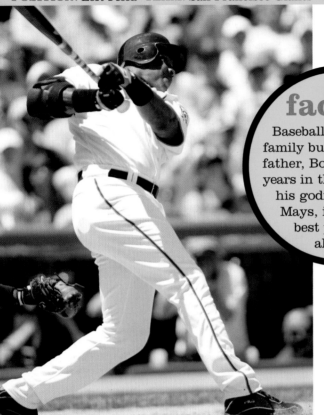

factoid

Baseball is the Bonds family business. Barry's father, Bobby, played 14 years in the Majors, and his godfather, Willie Mays, is one of the best players of all time.

Whenever Bonds retires, he will have some of the best career statistics in the history of the game. Over the years, he has been so dangerous with a bat in his hands that few pitchers have been willing to throw him anything he can swing at. He is patient, though, and on the rare occasion when a ball goes near the plate, Barry is always ready to jump on it. He hit a Big League-record 73 home runs in 2001. And in 2007, he was approaching Hank Aaron for the all-time mark of 755. Barry also has been a great outfielder, winning eight Gold Gloves. He even sets records in the off-season — he has won a record seven MVP Awards!

38 JASONBAY

How does a kid from Trail, British Columbia (in Canada, where hockey seems to be everyone's favorite sport), wind up playing baseball for a living? "When I got old enough," says Jason Bay, who spent his share of time on the ice as a kid, "I realized that I loved baseball." The Pirates are thankful for that. Bay has become their star player over the last few seasons. He was the 2004 National League Rookie of the Year and an All-Star in 2005 and '06. From the looks of it, he doesn't miss his skates one bit.

STAT CHART

Here's how Bay's rookie year stacks up against another great Canadian outfielder's first season in the Bigs:

LARRY WALKER (1990):
.241 AVG, 19 HR, 51 RBI

JASON BAY (2004):
.282 AVG, 26 HR, 82 RBI

POSITION: Left Field
TEAM: Pittsburgh Pirates
THROWS: Right BATS: Right
UNIFORM #: 38

POSITION: Shortstop **TEAM:** Philadelphia Phillies **THROWS:** Right **BATS:** Switch **UNIFORM #:** 11

Even on an infield with stars Chase Utley and Ryan Howard, Rollins gets plenty of attention. That's because he is a talented player who also is very fun to watch. Before the 2007 season, he got people talking when he said that his Phillies were the team to beat in the NL East. It was a bold thing to say since the team hadn't been to the playoffs since 1993, but it got Philadelphia excited and created a little more competition in the division. Early on, Jimmy did his part to make it come true, too. He hit 13 homers and stole 13 bases in his first 71 games.

STAT CHART

From August 2005 to April 2006, Rollins put together the eighth-longest hitting streak in history (38 games). His numbers during that stretch:

HOT STREAK:
.379 AVG (64 for 169), 15 SB, 23 RBI

❝ **It's a beautiful thing to see how talented he is now. Everybody who knew him knew he was destined to do great things.** ❞
—fellow Encinal (CA) High School graduate
Dontrelle Willis in *USA Today*

40 DERREK LEE

POSITION: First Base **TEAM:** Chicago Cubs **THROWS:** Right **BATS:** Right **UNIFORM #:** 25

Derrek Lee always was a very good Big League player, but in 2005, he took his game to new heights. "He's been something unbelievable," his All-Star teammate, Aramis Ramirez, said during that season. "Not many people can do what he's done." All he did was come close to a Triple Crown (which is when a player leads the league in homers, RBI and average). That doesn't happen often. He finished first in average (.335), second in home runs (46) and seventh in RBI (107). He's more than a hitter, too. "He's as good as they come defensively," says Derek Jeter. Although an injury cut Lee's 2006 season short, he returned to excellence again early in 2007.

41 DONTRELLE WILLIS

POSITION: Pitcher **TEAM:** Florida Marlins **THROWS:** Left **BATS:** Left **UNIFORM #:** 35

Dontrelle Willis uses one of the most unusual throwing motions in baseball today. It's also one of the most effective. He won the NL Rookie of the Year Award in 2003, when he was just 21 years old. That same year, he helped his team, the Marlins, win the World Series. Two years later, Dontrelle won 22 games to lead the National League. Born in Oakland, Calif., Willis is not only a good pitcher, he's also a fun person. He plays the game with energy and a smile, which is why so many people love to watch him.

factoid
Good thing Dontrelle is in the National League. He can hit nearly as well as he pitches. In 2006, he hit three home runs, including a grand slam in July.

42 TREVOR HOFFMAN

POSITION: Pitcher **TEAM:** San Diego Padres **THROWS:** Right **BATS:** Right **UNIFORM #:** 51

MAGIC NUMBER
500
Trevor is the first ever to reach 500 saves.

Trevor Hoffman has been closing games for the Padres since 1993, which is a long time to be with one franchise. The game's all-time saves leader, Hoffman led the National League with 53 saves in 1998, and he recorded career save No. 500 on June 6, 2007. Trevor's change-up is like a magic trick to Major League hitters. "That Hoffy change-up," says former Big Leaguer-turned-announcer Gary Matthews, "just disappears."

43 KEN GRIFFEY JR.

> **"I** mean, anyone who's around him sees that he hits and hits and hits. I don't know how he does it.**"**
>
> —former teammate Austin Kearns

"Player of the '90s" — that's a title that only one player can put on his resume: Ken Griffey Jr. Throughout the decade, Griffey played incredible baseball at the plate and in center field. He won an MVP Award in 1997. While Junior has had a tough time battling injuries in the 2000s, he is still capable of taking a pitcher deep and driving in runs. With a trophy case full of Gold Glove Awards, a ton of All-Star Game appearances and his continuing climb up the all-time home run list, Griffey is still a lock for the Hall of Fame. And with his outgoing personality and constant smile, Junior will always be a favorite among fans and teammates.

POSITION: Right Field
TEAM: Cincinnati Reds
THROWS: Left **BATS:** Left
UNIFORM #: 3

44 TORII HUNTER

POSITION: Center Field **TEAM:** Minnesota Twins **THROWS:** Right **BATS:** Right **UNIFORM #:** 48

There aren't too many players that people pay to watch on defense. As important as playing in the field is, it usually comes second to hitting in the minds of the fans. But it's different with Torii Hunter. They call him "Spiderman" because of the way he climbs the outfield wall. He seems to catch everything hit to center, and he won six straight Gold Gloves from 2001–06. Torii is very good at the plate, too, making him a well-balanced superhero.

STAT CHART

Torii does it at the plate and in the field.

	G	HR	RBI	AVG	Errors
2003:	154	26	102	.250	4
2004:	138	23	81	.271	4
2005:	98	25	56	.269	3
2006:	147	31	98	.278	4

45 CURTSCHILLING

POSITION: Pitcher
TEAM: Boston Red Sox
THROWS: Right
BATS: Right
UNIFORM #: 38

Schilling has had a great Big League career, and he was strong out of the gate in 2007. The Red Sox are his fifth team in 20 years of pitching. He has won more than 200 games over the years and two World Series rings. He will be remembered forever for his effort in Game 2 of the 2004 World Series, when he pitched through pain to beat St. Louis. Curt also is one of only nine players in baseball history born in the state of Alaska.

MAGIC NUMBER

20

Curt won 20-plus games in 2001, '02 and '04.

46 MATTHOLLIDAY

POSITION: Left Field
TEAM: Colorado Rockies
THROWS: Right **BATS:** Right
UNIFORM #: 5

After just three seasons, Matt Holliday was already a Big League star. The most impressive thing about him, though, is how much he improves every year. Matt had a very solid rookie season in 2004, when he hit .290 with 14 homers. The following year, his numbers went up in every category. The same thing happened in 2006, when his average jumped 19 points to .326 and he hit 15 more home runs. The start of 2007 was more of the same, and now everyone is taking notice.

factoid

At Stillwater (OK) High School, Matt was an All-American in both baseball and football. He was even recruited to be the quarterback for Oklahoma State.

47 ARAMIS RAMIREZ

POSITION: Third Base **TEAM:** Chicago Cubs **THROWS:** Right **BATS:** Right **UNIFORM #:** 16

Between 1974 and 2004, the Cubs used 100 different players at third base. "Hopefully, I can change all of that," Ramirez said early in his career in Chicago. Mission accomplished. After watching Ramirez have a terrific three years in which he hit 105 home runs, the Cubs signed him up for the long term.

factoid

Aramis was born in the capital of the Dominican Republic, Santo Domingo, just like other MLB Top 50 stars David Ortiz, Manny Ramirez and Albert Pujols.

48 BARRY ZITO

POSITION: Pitcher **TEAM:** San Francisco Giants **THROWS:** Left **BATS:** Left **UNIFORM #:** 75

When the Giants signed Barry Zito after the 2006 season, they got more than a great arm. They got a great thinker, too — a pitcher that knows how he has to approach his job in order to do his very best. "If you have a rock-solid concept of who you are and what you can achieve," he says, "then you're going to go places." Zito already has. The 2002 AL Cy Young winner clearly is one of the best around. His finest pitch is a looping curveball that has been fooling hitters since Zito started throwing it in Little League.

MAGIC NUMBER

0

Zito's career trips to the DL, entering 2007.

49 FELIX HERNANDEZ

POSITION: Pitcher **TEAM:** Seattle Mariners **THROWS:** Right **BATS:** Right **UNIFORM #:** 34

When he broke into the Majors on Aug. 4, 2005, Felix Hernandez, at age 19, was the youngest pitcher to throw in the Bigs in more than 20 seasons. That same year, *Baseball America* called him the No. 1 pitching prospect in the game. He is a special kind of talent, with such great stuff that he has been nicknamed "King Felix." In 2005, the King struck out 176 in 191 innings and won 12 games. Although he has a lot of experience, he's still in his early 20s and learning how to be an ace. When it does all come together, starts like his on Opening Day 2007 (when Felix threw eight shutout innings and struck out 12) could become common.

50 JOSHBECKETT

POSITION: Pitcher **TEAM:** Boston Red Sox **THROWS:** Right **BATS:** Right **UNIFORM #:** 19

" **I'm a confident guy. You've got to have some arrogance to be a professional pitcher.** "

—Josh Beckett

Josh Beckett is the last guy listed on the MLB Top 50, which is no insult. But when he's on, he's capable of pitching like he belongs in the Top 10. He was on right out of the gate in 2007, starting 10-1 with a 3.14 ERA in 13 starts and helping the Red Sox take a comfortable lead in the AL East.

If Boston is to get back to the World Series, Josh will probably play a big role. He has the experience, having sparked the Marlins to a World Series title in 2003. In that Series, Beckett went 1-1 with a 1.10 ERA to earn MVP honors. He won 41 games with Florida in five seasons before joining Boston.

THE TOPS

Here are some other "best of" lists to debate with your friends.

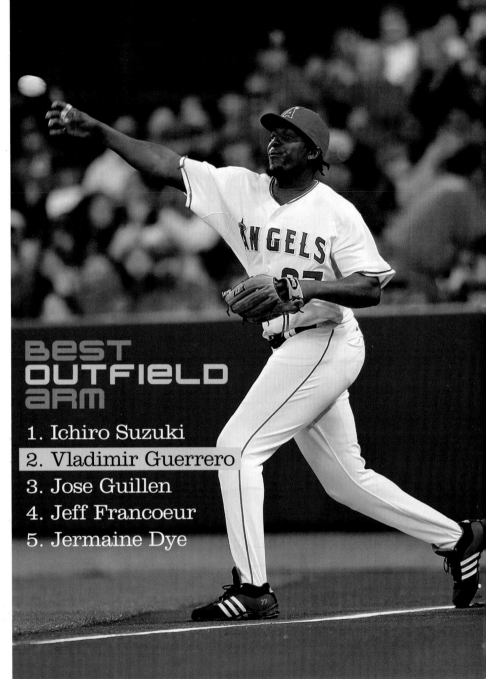

BEST OUTFIELD ARM

1. Ichiro Suzuki
2. Vladimir Guerrero
3. Jose Guillen
4. Jeff Francoeur
5. Jermaine Dye

HIGHEST BASEBALL IQ

1. Greg Maddux
2. Derek Jeter
3. Albert Pujols
4. Ivan Rodriguez
5. Jason Varitek ▲

TOP PLAYOFF HITTER

1. Derek Jeter
2. David Ortiz
3. Albert Pujols
◄ 4. Carlos Beltran
5. Chipper Jones

BEST
CURVE

1. Barry Zito ▶
2. Roy Oswalt
3. Ben Sheets
4. Roy Halladay
5. Felix Hernandez

BEST
BALLPARK

1. Wrigley Field
2. Fenway Park
3. PNC Park
4. AT&T Park ▼
5. Camden Yards

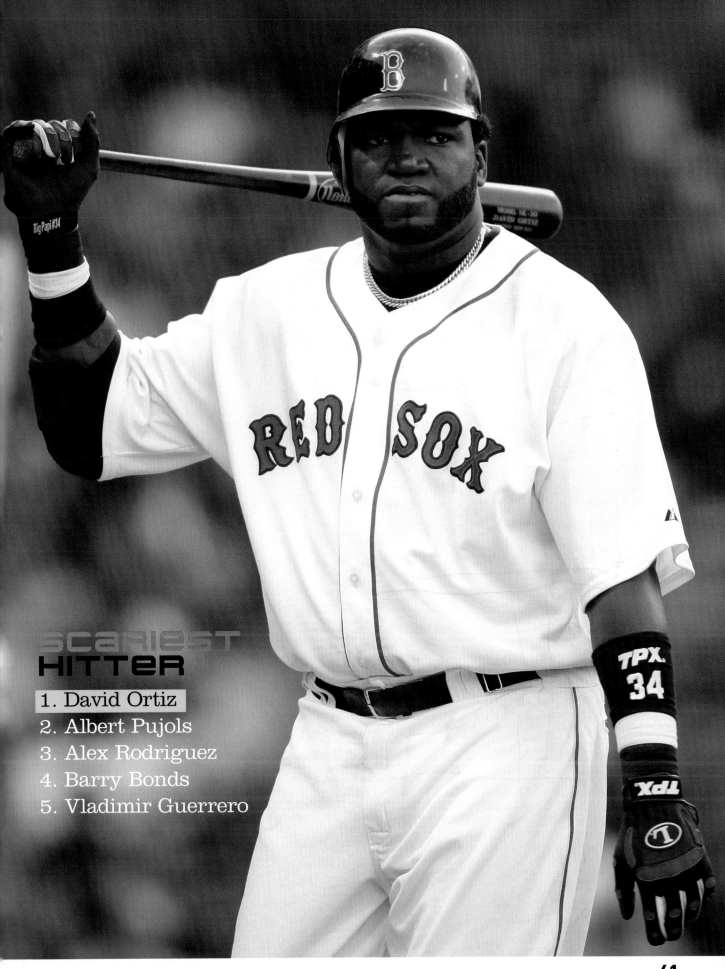

SCARIEST HITTER

1. David Ortiz
2. Albert Pujols
3. Alex Rodriguez
4. Barry Bonds
5. Vladimir Guerrero

BIGGEST JOKESTER

1. Nick Swisher
2. David Ortiz
3. Jose Reyes
4. Vernon Wells
5. Ken Griffey Jr.

Swisher (33)

IRONMAN

1. Miguel Tejada
2. Ichiro Suzuki
3. Michael Young
4. Barry Zito
5. Adam Dunn

DIRTIEST UNIFORM

1. Grady Sizemore
2. Jose Reyes
3. David Eckstein
4. Derek Jeter
5. Eric Byrnes

MOST ALL-STAR GAME SELECTIONS
(THROUGH 2007)

1. Ivan Rodriguez (14)
1. Barry Bonds (14)
3. Ken Griffey Jr. (13)
4. Mike Piazza (12)
5. Roger Clemens (11)
5. Manny Ramirez (11)
5. Alex Rodriguez (11)

BATTERTRACKER

PLAYER	SEASON	HR	RBI	AVG	SB
Alec	Thunder	O	3	.416	13

Now that you've read about Major League Baseball's Top 50 players, you should keep an eye on the box scores and stat sheets. Above is a grid to fill in the statistics of your favorite

PLAYER

PITCHER TRACKER

PLAYER	SEASON	W	ERA	K	SV
Alec	Hurtig	0-1	0.033	3	0

hitters and your favorite pitchers. Use these blank spaces to enter the name and numbers posted by these terrific players, or any other Major Leaguer that you'd like to follow.

TRACKER

WORDSEARCH

Hidden in the grid below are the last names of 15 of Major League Baseball's best pitchers. The names may be listed in all different directions: forward, backward, up, down and diagonally. How many can you find?

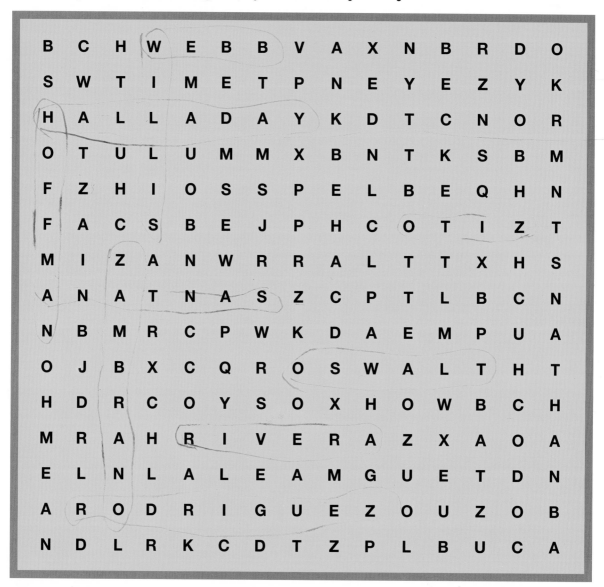

```
B C H W E B B V A X N B R D O
S W T I M E T P N E Y E Z Y K
H A L L A D A Y K D T C N O R
O T U L U M M X B N T K S B M
F Z H I O S S P E L B E Q H N
F A C S B E J P H C O T I Z T
M I Z A N W R R A L T T X H S
A N A T N A S Z C P T L B C N
N B M R C P W K D A E M P U A
O J B X C Q R O S W A L T H T
H D R C O Y S O X H O W B C H
M R A H R I V E R A Z X A O A
E L N L A L E A M G U E T D N
A R O D R I G U E Z O U Z O B
N D L R K C D T Z P L B U C A
```

(Josh) BECKETT
(Chris) CARPENTER
(Roy) HALLADAY
(Trevor) HOFFMAN
(Joe) NATHAN

(Roy) OSWALT
(Jonathan) PAPELBON
(Jake) PEAVY
(Mariano) RIVERA
(Francisco) RODRIGUEZ

(Johan) SANTANA
(Brandon) WEBB
(Dontrelle) WILLIS
(Carlos) ZAMBRANO
(Barry) ZITO

RECORDMATCHING

Match the Top 50 player on the left with the record he holds on the right.

1. Ichiro Suzuki	A. Most home runs by a second-year player
2. Mariano Rivera	B. Single-season home run record
3. Ryan Howard	C. Single-season hits record
4. Alfonso Soriano	D. Career postseason hits record
5. Alex Rodriguez	E. Youngest player to homer in a World Series game
6. Joe Mauer	F. All-time saves record
7. Trevor Hoffman	G. First 40-homer/40-double/40-steal season
8. Barry Bonds	H. First catcher to win an AL batting title
9. Derek Jeter	I. Most homers by a shortstop in a season
10. Andruw Jones	J. Career postseason saves record

HARDBALLTRIVIA

Now that you're all warmed up, it's time to really test your baseball knowledge. Below are some trivia questions about MLB's Top 50 players. You can find all of the answers somewhere in this book. How many can you get?

1. What young star became the first Canadian to win the AL MVP Award?

2. What AL closer was originally drafted as a shortstop?

3. What NL pitcher hit three home runs in 2006, including a grand slam?

4. What leadoff man put together a 38-game hitting streak from August 2005 to April 2006?

5. What veteran pitcher was born in Alaska?

6. Who is the only pitcher in Twins history to win more than one Cy Young Award?

7. What slugger has his own brand of salsa?

8. What active player won the Rookie of the Year and MVP awards in consecutive years?

9. Devil Rays outfielder Carl Crawford was once recruited to play basketball at what Pac-10 school?

10. What All-Star outfielder hails from the island of Curaçao?

BRACLSME (SCRAMBLE)

Below are the names of five of the best outfielders in all of Major League Baseball. The only catch is we've scrambled their names so the letters are out of order. How many can you unscramble?

1. OCASLR ERALBNT

_ _ _ _ _ _   _ _ _ _ _ _ _

2. IOTIR RUTHEN

_ _ _ _ _   _ _ _ _ _ _

3. NYMNA RZMERIA

_ _ _ _ _   _ _ _ _ _ _ _

4. LCRA WOFRACDR

_ _ _ _   _ _ _ _ _ _ _ _

5. TMTA DHLOYLIA

_ _ _ _   _ _ _ _ _ _ _ _

All answers on page 48.

WORDSEARCH

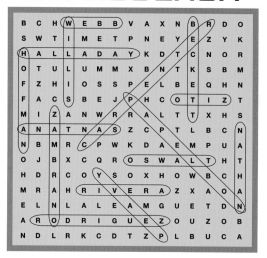

RECORD MATCHING

1-C	6-H
2-J	7-F
3-A	8-B
4-G	9-D
5-I	10-E

SCRAMBLE

1. Carlos Beltran
2. Torii Hunter
3. Manny Ramirez
4. Carl Crawford
5. Matt Holliday

HARDBALL TRIVIA

1. Justin Morneau
2. Joe Nathan
3. Dontrelle Willis
4. Jimmy Rollins
5. Curt Schilling
6. Johan Santana
7. David Ortiz
8. Ryan Howard
9. UCLA
10. Andruw Jones